1 MONTH OF FREE READING

at

www.ForgottenBooks.com

By purchasing this book you are eligible for one month membership to ForgottenBooks.com, giving you unlimited access to our entire collection of over 1,000,000 titles via our web site and mobile apps.

To claim your free month visit:
www.forgottenbooks.com/free1374172

ISBN 978-1-397-33029-1
PIBN 11374172

PHILADELPHIA

SOCIAL SCIENCE ASSOCIATION.

MANUAL TRAINING

—A—

Valuable Feature in General Education.

*Read at a Joint Meeting of the Philadelphia Social Science
Association and the Public Education Association.*

DECEMBER 11th, 1885,

BY

C. M. WOODWARD, Ph. D.

Director of the St. Louis Manual Training School.

Published by the
PHILADELPHIA SOCIAL SCIENCE ASSOCIATION,
720 Locust Street, Philadelphia.

The work of the Constitutional Convention. By A. Sydney Biddle.
What shall Philadelphia do with its Paupers? By Dr. Isaac Ray.
Proportional Representation. By S. Dana Horton.
Statistics Relating to Births, Deaths, Marriages, etc., in Philadelphia. By John Stockton Hough, M. D.
On the Value of Original Scientific Research. By Dr. Ruschenberger.
On the Relative Influence of City and Country Life on Morality, Health, Fecundity, Longevity, and Morality. By John Stockton Hough, M. D.
The Public School System of Philadelphia. By James S. Whitney.
The Utility of Government Geological Surveys. By Prof. J. P. Lesley.
The Law of Partnership. By J. G. Rosengarten.
Methods of Valuation of Real Estate for Taxation. By Thomas Cochran.
The Merits of Cremation. By Persifor Frazer, Jr.
Outlines of Penology. By Joseph R. Chandler.
Hygiene of the Eye, Considered with Reference to the Children in our Schools. By Dr. F. D. Castle.
The Relative Morals of City and Country. By William S. Pierce.
Silk Culture and Home Industry. By Dr. Samuel Chamberlaine.
Mind Reading, etc. By Persifor Frazer, Jr.
Legal Status of Married Women in Pennsylvania. By N. D. Miller.
The Revised Statutes of the United States. By Lorin Blodget.
Training of Nurses for the Sick. By John H. Packard, M. D.
The Advantages of the Co-operative Feature of Building Associations. By E. Wrigley.
The Operations of our Building Associations. By Joseph I. Doran.
Free Coinage and a Self-Adjusting Ratio. By Thomas Balch.
Building System for Great Cities. By Lorin Blodget.
Metric System. By Persifor Frazer, Jr.
Cause and Cure of Hard Times. By R. J. Wright.
House-Drainage and Sewerage. By George E. Waring, Jr.
A Plea for a State Board of Health. By Benjamin Lee, M. D.
The Germ-Theory of Disease, and its Present Bearing upon Public and Personal Hygiene. By Joseph G. Richardson, M. D.
Technical Education. By A. C. Rembaugh, M. D.
The English Methods of Legislation Compared with the American. By S. Sterne.
Thoughts on the Labor Question. By Rev. D. O. Kellogg.
On the Isolation of Persons in Hospitals for the Insane. By Dr. Isaac Ray.
Philadelphia Charity Organization. By Rev. Wm. H. Hodge.
Public Schools in their Relations to the Community. By James S. Whitney.
Industrial and Decorative Art in Public Schools. By Charles G. Leland.
Penal and Reformatory Institutions. By J. G. Rosengarten.
Nominations for Public Office. By Mayer Sulzberger.
Municipal Government. By John C. Bullitt.
Apprenticeship as it Was and Is. By Addison B. Burk.
The American Aristocracy. By Lincoln L. Eyre.
A Plea for a New City Hospital. By Thomas W. Barlow.
The Pending School Problems. By Professor M. B. Snyder.
Municipal Government. By Wm Righter Fisher.
Social Condition of the Industrial Classes. By Lorin Blodget.
Progress of Industrial Education. By Philip C. Garrett.
A Plea for Better Distribution. By Charles M. Du Puy.
Milk Supply of our Large Cities. etc., etc. By J. Cheston Morris, M. D.
Alcohol. By A. C. Rembaugh
Sanitary Influence of Forest Growth. Dr. J. M. Anders
Outline of a Proposed School of Political and Social Science. By Edmund J. James, Ph. D.
The Organization of Local Boards of Health in Pennsylvania. By Benj. Lee, A. M., M. D., Ph. D.
Manual Training a Valuable Feature in General Education. By C. M. Woodward, Ph. D.

MANUAL TRAINING A FEATURE IN
GENERAL EDUCATION.

Forty years ago Ralph Waldo Emerson charged popular education with a want of truth and nature. He complained that an education to things was not given. He saw that literature, far from being the only factor in civilization, was not even the chief one. Said he: "We are students of words; we are shut up in schools and colleges and recitation rooms for 10 or 15 years, and come out at last with a bag of wind, a memory of words, and do not know a thing. We cannot use our hands, or our legs, or our eyes, or our arms." And again, speaking of the exclusive devotion of schools to Latin, Greek and pure mathematics, "which by a wonderful drowsiness of usage" had been "stereotyped education," he says: "In a hundred high schools and colleges, this warfare against common sense still goes on."

This man of clear vision pointed out the road which the next generation was to follow. With wonderful unanimity the educational forces of America are facing in the new direction. Formal education is much broader than of old, and the methods and materials used are so new or so changed that we call the result the

NEW EDUCATION.

It is scarcely necessary to add that the "new" education includes the "old." We tear down no essential parts of the old temple, but we have added at least two wings which were needed to make a symmetrical whole. The natural science wing brings in a whole world of new material, and a totally new method of developing ideas. The other wing is that of manual training, including a variety of drawing and the intelligent use of a large range of typical tools and materials.

"Man," says Carlyle, "is a tool-using animal. He can use tools, can devise tools; with these the granite mountains melt into light dust before him; he kneads glowing iron as if it were

(3)

soft paste; seas are his smooth highway, winds and fire his unwearying steeds. Nowhere do you find him without tools; without tools, he is nothing; with tools, he is all."

You know how bird-trainers teach a canary to sing a particular tune. The poor bird is put in a dark place, where he can see nothing of interest, and then compel him to hear the tune and nothing else. Even a bird is constrained to a certain amount of intellectual activity and in sheer desperation he sings the only thing he is allowed to think of. Have we not been training our boys too much on the same plan? Have we not walled in their vision till they could look only in certain directions, see certain activities, study certain forms of mental life? Half the occupations of men, half the domains of knowledge, many of the means and ends of intellectual culture, much that is specially favorable to moral and spiritual growth, is beyond their horizon. Need any one be surprised at the result of such seclusion? Like the bird, they learn certain tongues, they master certain arts, they become familiar with a certain limited round of intellectual life. There is little freedom of choice or chance for liberal growth. They must, perforce, travel certain paths. And, later on, they think, and for the most part with good reason, that to use their education—by which they mean their book knowledge—they must go into the counting room, become salesmen, or go into the "learned professions." In avoiding, with almost perfect unanimity, the mechanic arts, they do not make an intelligent choice; they follow only an ignorant prejudice. Now, this evil of narrowness, this "violation" of the "rights" of children, as Prof. Felix Adler calls it, is what we are trying to cure by the introduction of the manual elements.

EXCELLENCE OF OUR COMMON SCHOOLS.

Let me be just to the bridge that has brought us over; to the ladder we have ourselves climbed. The schools need no defender—they speak for themselves. To the public schools of Massachusetts I owe more than I can ever pay. From the door of a country high school I stepped up to the college gate, as thousands of boys have done since. Far be it from me to say an unkind or disloyal word of the common school system. The schools of Massachusetts are the brightest jewel in her crown, the sure anchor of her hope. The high standard of your patriotism and good citizenship is evidence enough of the excellence of your system of public instruction.

But does not the world move? Does it not become the school master to keep step to the notes of progress? Shall the demands of the age greatly change? Shall we depart wisely from the ways of our fathers in everything else, in our industries, our amusements, in the circumstances and surroundings of our homes, and make no change in the content of our school education? That the education afforded has in the main been judicious and fairly complete I do not call in question.

While I think it altogether probable that throughout all grades there is too much of committing to memory the words, statements and conclusions of others as mere facts to be remembered for their own sake, and too little practice in getting at knowledge for one's self and drawing one's own conclusions, under the guidance, but not at the command, of the teacher, I shall confine my remarks to-night to what we are doing, or ought to do, for boys and girls from the age of, say, 13 to 17 or 18. I say girls, as well as boys, for I believe that they equally need manual training. Much that is serviceable for boys is equally so for the girls; much has yet to be done in developing the details. Insist that some manual training should run through the entire course from the kindergarten to the high school. The necessary appliances for the primary and grammar grades are simple and few, the most essential thing being teachers, into whose preparatory training manual elements have entered in their due proportion. By the eighth or ninth year of school life, the pupils are ready for the systematic and comprehensive work I am about to describe.

THE DAILY PROGRAMME.

The school time of the pupils is about equally divided between mental and manual exercises. The daily session begins at 9 A. M. and closes at 3.30 P. M., 30 minutes being allowed for lunch. Each pupil has daily three recitations, one hour of drawing and two hours of shop practice.

THE COURSE OF INSTRUCTION

covers three years, and embraces five parallel lines, three purely intellectual and two both intellectual and manual, as follows:

First—A course of pure mathematics, including arithmetic, algebra, geometry and plane trigonometry.

Second—A course in science and applied mathematics, including physical geography, botany, natural philosophy, chemistry, mechanics, mensuration and book-keeping.

Third—A course in language and literature, including English grammar, spelling, composition, literature, history and the elements of political science and economy. Latin and French are introduced as electives with English or science.

Fourth—A course in penmanship, free-hand and mechanical drawing.

Fifth—A course of tool instruction, including carpentry, wood turning, moulding, brazing, soldering, forging, and bench and machine work in metals.

Students have no option or election as to particular studies, except as regards Latin and French; each must conform to the course as laid down and take every branch in its order.

A BROADER EDUCATION.

You will see, then, that we have no mean or narrow object. " The education which the manual training school represents is a broader, and not, as the opponents of the new education assert, a narrower education." We put the whole boy to school, not a part of him, and we train him by the most invigorating and logical methods. We believe that mental activity and growth are closely allied to physical activity and growth, and that each is secured more readily and more fully in connection with the other than by itself.

There can be no question as to the value of language and letters, of books and literary methods in general education. No science can exist without letters. We only insist that neither as an end nor as a means does literature, even with the aid of pure mathematics, supply more than half the needs of a healthy education.

Pure literature is a matter of books alone. It deals with words and symbols, and is concerned only with the forms of verbal expression. The thought expressed may belong to any department of science or philosophy ; to psychology, botany or metaphysics ; to religion, history, technology or art ; the form belongs to literature, and it may be in the language of any people. The matter of form is in the realm of authority, and everything is settled by an appeal to authorities. The conventions of society are such that too often education is gauged by the amount of literary culture involved. We are the slaves of fashion in education as well as in dress, and often fear to claim for other kinds of culture, as useful, as humane, as invigorating, as broadly healthful, as that of letters, the value and dignity they really possess. In defence of the new education, it has been said that "the intellectual culture of active art is far more vigorous than that of literature. In literary culture, we feebly and indefinitely grasp ideas by their association with printed words. There is no life, no force in the object of our study. In industrial art, we are continually stimulated by the presence of the object, and the operations we are performing, and our perceptions are clear, positive and exact. The concentrated attention, the close observation, the ingenuity, invention and judgment in use in art are far superior as mental discipline to any that literature can give."

The study of science in the new education involves both new materials and new methods. The unfruitfulness of all attempts to teach a child science, in which at first there should be no such thing as authority, from a book, as would be the case for a language where authority is everything, has produced a revolution in science teaching. But the science laboratory is a work-shop as well, and success there depends in part upon manual skill in the use of tools, in mechanical processes, and in the graphic arts. Moreover, we believe that

HEALTHY GROWTH IS ALWAYS PLEASURABLE,

whether of mind or body. We believe that it is no more necessary to give the mind disagreeable, wearisome, unintelligible exercises than it is to give the body disgusting, ill-assorted, indigestible food. Did you ever see one whose mind was nauseated with spelling books, lexicons and grammars, and an endless hash of words and definitions? And did you, in such a case, call in the two doctors, Johann Pestallozzi and Friedrich Frœbel? And did you watch the magic influence of a diet of things prescribed by the former in the place of words, and a little vigorous practice in doing, in the place of talking, under the direction of the latter?

When the limit of sharp attention and lively interest is reached, you have reached the limit of profitable study. If you can hold the attention of a class but 10 minutes, it is worse than a waste of time to make the exercise 15. The weary intellects will roll themselves up in self-defence, and suffer as patiently as they can, but the memory of those moments of torture lingers and throws its dreadful shadow over the exercise as it comes up again on the morrow; and how automatically, as these over-taught children take their places again, do they roll themselves up into an attitude of mental stupidity. Intellectual growth is not to be gauged by the length or number of the daily recitations. I firmly believe that in most of our schools there is too much sameness and monotony, too much intellectual weariness and consequent torpor.

A moment's reflection will convince you that the ordinary secondary school, whether high school or academy, does not meet the general want of 13 and 15 year old boys. The curriculum of studies is laid out for that very limited class of pupils who are destined, or self-selected without intelligent choice, for literary or professional life. With all that work I have no wish to interfere. I would even raise all professional and literary standards. I would incorporate with their study of classics and mathematics and authoritative science such a manual training as would make them better literary and professional men.

MUCH MORE THAN MEMORY.

But I would do much more. I would make school attractive and indespensable to a large class of boys whose controlling interests are not in the study of words, the forms of speech or the boundless mass of information which is given in books; and I would give such boys a fair chance of adequate development. Such boys are not necessarily blockheads, nor even dull. Their intellectual powers may be strong, though their strength lies not in the direction of memory. The claims of this class of boys have been set forth by no one so eloquently as by Gen. Francis A. Walker. Says he, and I give almost his exact words: "There is now no place, or only a most uncomfortable one, for those boys who are strong in perception, apt in manipulation, and correct in the interpretation of phenomena, but who are not good at memorizing, or rehearsing the opinions and statements of others; or who, by their diffidence or slowness of speech are unfitted for ordinary intellectual gymnastics. These boys are quite as numerous as the other sort, and are quite as deserving of sympathy and respect, beside being rather better qualified to become of use in the industrial and social order. And yet for this class of boys the school offers almost nothing upon which they can employ their priceless powers. They may, by laboring very painfully over the prescribed, but uncongenial, exercises, escape the stigma of being blockheads, but they can never do very well in them. They will always appear to disadvantage when compared with the boys with good memories for words, whose mental and moral natures accept with pleasure or without serious question the statements and conclusions of others. Such boys are practically ploughed under in our schools, as not worth harvesting. And yet it not infrequently happens that the boy who is regarded as dull because he cannot master an artificial system of grammatical analysis; isn't worth a cent for giving a list of the Kings of England; doesn't know and doesn't care what are the principal productions of Borneo—has a better pair of eyes, a better pair of hands, a better judgment, and even by the standards of the merchant, the manufacturer and the railroad president, a better head than his master."

Now the manual training school proposes to cultivate and

HARVEST BOTH KIND OF BOYS.

As Col. Jacobson says: "Manual training means not fewer, but more ladies and gentlemen to the acre."

Hence, if we abridge, in some cases, the hours given to books and the time wasted in idleness, and introduce exercises of a widely different character, the result is a positive intellectual gain. There is plenty of time if you will but use it aright. The students of a well-conducted manual training school are intellectually as active and vigorous as in any high school. Nay, more, I claim, and I have had good opportunity to observe the facts, that even on the intellectual side the manual training boy has a decided advantage. I have been in charge of both kinds of school, and I know whereof I speak. The education of the hand is the means of more completely and efficaciously educating the brain.

INTELLECTUAL VALUE.

Manual exercises, which are at the same time intellectual exercises, are highly attractive to healthy boys. If you doubt this, go in to the shops of a manual training school and see for yourselves. Go, for instance, into our forging shop, where metals are wrought through the agency of heat. A score of young Vulcans, bare-armed, leather-aproned, with many a drop of honest sweat, stand up to their anvils with an unconscious earnestness which shows how much they enjoy their work. What are they doing? They are using brains and hands. They are studying definitions in the only dictionary which really defines. Where else can they learn the meaning of such words as "iron," "steel," "welding," "tempering," "upsetting," "chilling," etc? And in the shop where metals are wrought cold (which, for want of a better name, we call our machine shop), every new exercise is like a delightful trip into a new field of thought and investigation. Every exercise, if properly conducted, is both mental and manual. Every tool used and every process followed has its history, its genesis, its evolution. Says Supt. Seaver: "Manual training is essential to the right and full development of the human mind, and, therefore, no less beneficial to those who are not going to become artisans than to those who are. The workshop method of instruction is of great educational value, for it brings the learner face to face with the facts of nature; his mind increases in knowledge by direct personal experience with forms of matter, and manifestations of force. No mere words intervene. The manual exercises of the shop train mental power rather than load the memory; they fill the mind with the solid merchandise of knowledge, and not with its empty packing-cases."

Supt. Dowd, of the Toledo public schools, says: "It is certainly true that the training of the manual training school lets in a flood of light upon a thousand things but imperfectly understood before."

Manual dexterity is but the evidence of a certain kind of mental power. Certain intellectual faculties, such as observation and judgment in inductive reasoning, cannot be properly trained except through the instrumentality of the hand. The proverbial caution of the practical manipulator and his distrust of mere theory—which means reasoning based on assumed, not real facts—show how unsafe is reasoning not founded on the closest observation and intimate knowledge of the facts of nature.

A manual training school does not stop with the training of the hand. Physical dexterity is but one, and the very least, of the many things sought, and this is sought more as a means than as an end. The great end is education ; the development of the mind and body, the simultaneous culture of the intellectual, physical and moral faculties. We believe in the study of

THINGS FIRST, THEIR SYMBOLS SECOND.

I am almost ready to say, "Confusion to the memory of Sam Johnson," for since he started the fashion of making dictionaries, pupils have been set to learn about substances, products and processes from dictionaries rather than from things themselves. When we reflect that every verb in the dictionary relies for its meaning to us upon our personal experience in being, doing and suffering, we shall realize something of the importance which personal physical experience bears to education.

The first step of the new education was the introduction of explanatory pictures and diagrams in the books studied and read. This was a great gain, and many of our illustrated text-books are to-day marvels of excellence. As books they leave little to be desired. But words, neither alone nor with pictures, can supply the want of things themselves. Next came the introduction of apparatus and models which the teacher could handle and show to his pupils, and sometimes, if he knew how, could use before them. The lecture method was another important gain, and it has accomplished much good. The difficulties attending it, however, have been such as to prevent its general adoption, and its use has been limited to schools of high grade.

The next step, and the one we are now taking, is the adoption of

THE LABORATORY,

the putting of things, materials, apparatus, tools and machines into the hands of the pupils themselves, and giving them a conscious knowledge of properties, relations and processes. This is the crowning feature in education. It is manifest on the one side in the kindergarten ; on the other, in the physical, chemical and dynamic laboratories ; while between the two come the shops and laboratories and drawing rooms of the manual training school. In this last named school we strive to get the benefit of all the progress made. We aim to have the best text books, the best illustrations, the best apparatus, the best shop and tools and the best teachers.

Milton recognized but five professions open to educated youth, viz : those of the theologian, the lawyer, the statesman, the soldier and the gentleman—the last being defined by him as one " who retires himself to the enjoyments of ease and luxury." On the other hand, J. Scott Russell, one of the first of England's educated and practical men, enumerates in his plan of an English technical university, after excluding theology, law and medicine, twenty-two modern professions, for which, in some way, education is to be provided.

MODERN PROFESSIONS.

It was formerly supposed that the manufacturer the miner, the builder of houses, or bridges, or ships, the millwright, the farmer, the man of commerce, etc., needed no education beyond that gained by actual work at his trade or desk. Now, however, such strides have been taken in all these callings, through the application of the principles of modern science, that none but carefully trained and educated men can expect to secure and keep places of honor and profit in them.

Now, without neglecting to train our lawyers, engineers and physicians, literary men and gentlemen of leisure, should we not at least as directly aim to train these other men for their work?

But some fellow-teacher will at once answer: "That is just what we have done. The training we give is of universal value; we aim to prepare equally for all honorable careers, to elevate and purify and ennoble the whole life." True, you do so aim, and I honor you for it. I can aim at nothing higher or better. But do you succeed as you should? Is your course of training just what it would be if all the St. Paul boys of high school age were all in the high school? Is not the absence of seven-eighths of these boys proof that your training does not cover the whole ground?

We want an education that shall develop the whole man. All his intellectual, moral and physical powers should be drawn out, and trained and fitted for doing good service in the battle of life. We want

WISE HEADS AND SKILLFUL HANDS.

There has been a growing demand, not only for men of knowledge, but for men of skill, in every department of human activity. Have our schools and colleges and universities been equal to the demand? Are we satisfied with what they have produced?

There is a wide conviction of the inutility of schooling for the great mass of children beyond the primary grades, and this conviction is not limited to any class or grade of intelligence. According to the report of the president of the Chicago school board, about one and one-eighth per cent. of the boys in the public schools are in the high schools. From his figures it appears that, if every boy in the Chicago public schools should extend his schooling through a high school, the four classes of the high schools would contain some 9000 boys ; in point of fact, they have about 400. Has the school board of Chicago done its full duty to the 8600 boys who are old enough to be in the high schools and yet are not there ?

If a manual training school could draw in 400 more of them, would it be worth the doing ?   I think it would a hundred fold.

ONE OUT OF ONE HUNDRED AND EIGHT.

Supt. Hinsdale, of Cleveland, says : " Of 108 pupils (boys and girls) entering the primary school, 60 complete the primary, 20 finish the grammar, four are found in the second class of the high, and one graduates from the high school." In St. Louis, the average age at which pupils withdraw from the public schools is 13½ years.   This is just the age when two or three years of " all-round " training may be of infinite value.

From the observed influence of manual training upon boys and, indirectly, upon the parents, I am led to claim that, when the last year of the grammar and the high schools include manual training, they will meet a wider demand ; that the education they afford will be really more valuable, and, consequently, that the attendance of boys will be more than doubled. Add the manual elements with their freshness and variety, their delightful shop exercise, their healthy intellectual and moral atmosphere, and the living reality of their work, and the boys will stay in school. Such a result would be an unmixed good. I have seen boys doing well in a manual training school, who could not have been forced to attend an ordinary school.

I well know how firmly fixed is the present curriculum of study in the secondary schools, by how many traditions it is supported, and how unfamiliar and strange the manual elements appear to our present corps of teachers.

But let me assure them that the manual exercises are in no way demoralizing.   Every shop and drawing room, like every other laaboratory, is a part of the school.   Boys go from mathematics to shop, and from shop to Latin or English as naturally as from mathematics direct to Latin.   Shop work is not play, though nineteen out of twenty boys enjoy it as heartily.   All the work is logically arranged, and simultaneous class exercises are rigidly insisted on. The difficulties of keeping a class together are no greater than they are in physics and chemistry.

Some of the things said about us are marked by a great lack of appreciation of our methods and results. For instance, an Illinois professor said a few years ago that hammering wood was such a different matter from hammering iron that not only was skill in one branch of no value in the other, but that it was a positive hindrance. At once the argument was caught up by the opponents of manual training, and we were entertained by learned discussions of the various arts of hammering by those who really knew nothing about them. It is as though one should insist that a knowledge of French is a hindrance to the learning of Spanish, or a knowledge of Latin an obstacle to the mastery of Greek. It is asserted that there can be no such thing as a general training in the use of tools, and they point to the cramped muscles and unintelligent automatonism of a man, who for years has headed pins or stamped small pieces of tin, as exhibiting the baneful effects of manual training! Is it possible that such people know what we mean by manual training?

THE HABIT OF THINKING.

Can they be aware that, in no American manual training school (and there are no such schools in France or Germany or Russia), is the number of hours devoted to the entire series of wood working tools over 400? That the stage of mechanical habit is never reached? That the only habit actually acquired is that of thinking? That no blow is struck, no line drawn, no motion regulated, from muscular habit? That the quality of every act springs from the conscious will accompanied by a definite act of judgment? Can such a limited training produce a high degree of manual skill? Of course not. We have distinctly stated that our pupils do not become skilled mechanics, nor do we teach them the full details of a single trade. The tools whose theory, care, and use we teach are representative, and the processes which we teach just far enough to make every step clear and experimentally understood, equally underlie a score of trades. I say experimentally understood, by which I mean that it is not enough to know that a certain outline is to be produced

or a certain adaptation is to be secured, but one must know just
the force to be directed, just the motions needed, and in their
order, and all as the result of the closest attention and steady
intellectual activity.

What then is this so-called manual training but continuous
mental discipline ? I have already spoken of the mental effect
of science study. I claim equally beneficial effects for the
thoughtful study of the theory and use of the tools which are
the product of ages of human experience.

OBJECT OF MANUAL TRAINING.

The object of the introduction of manual training is not to
make mechanics. I have said that many times, and I find con-
tinual need of repeating the statement. We teach banking, not
because we expect our pupils to become bankers ; and we teach
drawing, not because we expect to train architects, or artists or
engineers ; and we teach the use of tools, the properties of
materials and the methods of the arts, not because we expect
our boys to become artizans. We teach them the United States
constitution and some of the acts of Congress, not because we
expect them all to become congressmen. But we do expect that
our boys will at least have something to do with bankers, and
architects, and artists, and engineers, and artizans, and we
expect all to become good citizens. Our great object is educational ; other objects are secondary. That industrial results
will surely follow I have not the least doubt, but they will take
care of themselves. Just as a love for the beautiful follows a
love for the true ; and, as the high arts cannot thrive except on
the firm foundation of the low ones, so a higher and finer
development of all industrial standards is sure to follow a rational
study of the underlying principles and methods. Every object
of attention put into the school-room should be put there for
two reasons, one educational or (to use a word I much dislike)
pedagogic, the other economic. Training, culture, skill come
first ; knowledge about persons, things, places, customs, tools,
methods, come second. It is only by securing both objects that
the pupil gains the great prize, which is power to deal succes-
fully with the men, things and activities which surround him.

THE ECONOMIC VALUE.

Now one word more on the secondary object, the economic. Some have not only failed to recognize the great educational value of manual training, but they have, as it seems to me, taken a too narrow view of its economic bearing. For instance, in analyzing the economic value of our shop work and drawing, Dr. Harris does not appear to think them of value to the farmer. Remember, it is not proposed to substitute manual training for any of the schooling the farmer's boy now receives. I cheerfully grant that all he gets is of value. I say add the manual training to his present curriculum. Will he not be the better farmer? Will it be of value to him to know how to repair a window, to hang a door, to plan and frame and erect a barn, to mend his plough, or harrow, to supply a bolt, or nut, or a missing link on his reaper or mowing machine? or to keep in order a windmill or a farm wagon? You, who draw such forcible figures of speech from the operations of a farm, will surely agree with me that to be successful a farmer must join the skillful hand to the cultured mind. I could tell you of many instances in which my own graduates have astonished the natives by stepping forward on an Illinois farm in the presence of half a score of able bodied men and speedily mending a break which had threatened to entail a half-day's idleness for the whole force.

I recently heard of a successful dentist in New York, who attributed his success to the training he had received when a boy in a general repair shop. Again, a noted surgeon says that his ability to make his own tools, was the basis of his success. A graduate of mine went into a factory for turning corn-cob pipes and stems, in Washington, Missouri. In a few days he ranked with any of the fifty men in the shop. Then he saw a possible improvement in the tools to be used. With a new tool, which he made himself, he was able soon to about double his productive power.

The habit of working on an exact plan, of analyzing an apparently complicated operation into a series of simple steps, enables one to solve many a new problem, even with new material and under entirely novel circumstances.

THE MORAL INFLUENCE.

A word in regard to the moral effect of our combination. Its influence is wholesome in three ways:

1. It stimulates a love for intellectual honesty. It deals with the substance, as well as with the shadow; it gives opportunity for primitive judgments; it shows in the concrete, in the most unmistakable form, the vast difference between right and wrong; it substitutes personal experience and the use of simple, forcible language, for the experience of others expressed in high sounding phrase. It associates the deed with the thought; the real with the ideal, and lays the foundation for honesty in thought and in act.

2. The good moral effect of occupation is most marked. No boys were ever so busy as ours, in school and out. Every strong, healthy appetite finds its appropriate food. The variety of the daily programme, far from confusing, produces a balance of healthy interests, and not only the boy's time, but his thoughts are devoted to the work of the school. The correlation of drawing and shop work with science and mathematical studies is exceedingly helpful on both sides, and parents testify to the absorption of our pupils in their work. Mothers and sisters are never tired of telling of the great convenience of having in the house one who has common sense enough to use the universal tools and to keep things in order. The hands are rarely idle enough to allow the devil to get in his mischievous work.

3. A third moral benefit is self-respect and a respect for honest, intelligent labor. A boy who sees nothing in manual labor but mere brute force despises both the labor and the laborer. To him all hand work is drudgery, and all men who use their hands are to him equally uncultivated and unattractive. With the acquisition of skill in himself comes a pride in its possession, and the ability and willingness to recognize it in his fellows. When once he appreciates skill in handicraft or in any manual art, he regards the possessor of it with sympathy and respect.

Without going into the perplexing questions of labor and capital, I feel sure that the only way to prevent such conflicts in the future is to properly train the children of the present generation. The men who make up mobs are deficient in either mental or manual training, or both. They never had a chance to get both side by side in a public or private school.

DIRECTIVE WORK.

But there is a higher view of even the economic side of the question. Mr. Edward Carpenter, speaking to the people of England of what Englishmen must do if they are to maintain their position at the head of the industrial world, thus refers to what we have called "directive" power.

"Administrative work has to be done in a nation as well as productive work; but it must be done by men accustomed to manual labor, who have the healthy decision and primitive authentic judgment which come of that, else it cannot be done well. In the new form of society which is slowly advancing upon us, this will be felt more than now. The higher the position of trust a man occupies, the more will it be thought important that, at some period of his life, he should have been thoroughly inured to manual work. This is not only on account of the physical and moral robustness implied by it, but equally because it will be seen to be impossible for any one, without this experience of what is the very flesh and blood of national life, to promote the good health of the nation, or to understand the conditions under which the people live whom he has to rule. Above all things have done with this ancient sham of fleeing from manual labor, of despising, or pretending to despise, it."

But some one will tell me that there is nothing new in manual training, that there have been countless manual labor experiments in this country, which have always failed; and that throughout Europe industrial schools have been in successful operation for thirty years. Now, those who thus object do not recognize essential differences. Let me clear up this very important matter.

. The so-called

"MANUAL LABOR" SCHOOLS

have been founded as semi-charitable institutions. They have been attempts to solve the problem: How shall a poor boy be enabled to earn his living and get his education at the same time? In my judgment there is no solution to that problem, and the sooner we recognize the fact that a good education costs money, and that every attempt to shift the burden of support upon children under seventeen years of age we are guilty of cruelty and neglect. Of necessity, the form of labor adopted in these labor schools is that which involves a minimum of training and skill and a quick return. The pupils learn some of the elements of a narrow occupation, but on the whole their education, whether mental or manual, is between very narrow limits. Such institutions have few points in common with a manual training school.

As to the

INDUSTRIAL SCHOOLS

of Europe, we all know they are intended to foster certain established industries. In a strictly "industrial" school, a single industry is taught, and with the definite and perfectly well understood object of making artisans in the industry taught. To be sure, there have been widespread efforts to improve the skill and value of the artisans by the introduction of some drawing and a minimum of science and mathematics, and with marked success. In Europe there is no feeling against such institutions, nor would there be here in a commercial establishment. In Europe the son of a miner goes to the mines, as a matter of course, and the son of a weaver has generally no hope beyond the loom. Except in rare instances, the child of a European laborer runs smoothly in grooves cut for him before he was born.

In America the case is quite different. A public school must put no bar to a boy's development; the upward roads are always to be left open. A public "trade school" in America would be out of place.

APPRENTICESHIP SCHOOLS.

There are in Europe many apprenticeship schools, which are generally of a higher grade than the industrial, and which have a somewhat broader aim, though in every case the definite object is to make every boy who attends, no matter what his natural aptitude, a skilled, practical mechanic. The literary and scientific training is in every case very limited, and the drawing is supposed to be directed to the wants of a single craft. As is too often the case with us, it is assumed that it requires no great amount of brains or intelligence to be a mechanic, and that intellectual culture is wasted on a man who finds employment for his hands. The broader aim I spoke of consists in furnishing a year of somewhat general training in which a boy may test his liking for several trades, one of which is to be selected at the end of the first year. They have no place for one who does not wish to enter upon a special trade. During a visit last May to an excellent apprenticeship school in Paris, after visiting every shop, drawing and recitation room and inspecting the daily programme of each section, I suggested to the director that I saw no provision for one who should prefer a general course for the entire three years. He wheeled upon me with the emphatic reply : " This is a school to make mechanics. Every boy here must be a mechanic. He must earn his living by his trade the moment he leaves this school."

A DIFFERENT THING.

Now, neither the American manual labor school, nor the European industrial school, nor the apprenticeship school comes very near the manual training school. With them either self-support or a trade is the great, and nearly the sole, end. The trade schools have a worthy end, and they are successful. They have greatly improved the grade of technical skill in Europe, and they have accomplished much for their industries. I have no opposition to make to them, but I wish it to be well understood that a manual training school is quite a different thing. Instead of the two grand objects we have in view—one general and educational, the other economic—they have but one, the economic.

In our school the manual elements are subordinated to the intellectual. One hour of drawing and two hours of shopwork daily is the maximum demand on the manual side. On the other

side, there are three recitation hours and private study enough
to learn three lessons.

THE CULTIVATION OF THE HUMANITIES.

All the hand work, like all the book work, is as "human"
as possible. Not every tool, not every book, not every art, not
every science is crowded into our curriculum. We teach a few
things, and we try to teach them well. I think we have introduced enough to secure the development of power.

TWO FALLACIES.

Two old fallacies have stood in our way, and they stand yet
in many minds. One is that all the manual arts, except penmanship and free-hand drawing, should be learned at home or
in connection with some business establishment. They always
have been so learned, it is urged, if learned at all, and there is
no good reason to suppose that they can be acquired to any
useful extent in any other way. Certainly they cannot be taught
in school.

There is little need for me to answer this objection here in
Boston. It has been answered in many ways. It has been
proved a hundred times that the logical methods of the school-
room are as applicable to the theory and use of tools and imple-
ments as to chemistry or algebra or book-keeping, and that no
business establishment is willing to train a boy solely in the
boy's interest. Superintendent MacAlister of Philadelphia, says
that needlework (*i. e.* plain sewing) is more logically taught than
is arithmetic in his school. I can say as much for what we teach
at the bench, the anvil, and the lathe. I have yet to find one
person who has looked closely into this matter, who does not
agree with me in this.

THE FALLACY OF SELF-SUPPORT.

The other fallacy is that the moment one introduces manual
training, he must bring in the idea of self-support. The notion
is inherited. Every apprentice boy, every counting-house fag
was supposed to pay for his training by his labor. So every

stranger who looks in upon our school asks what we do with the boys' work; and, can we not make things to sell?

They forget, in the first place, that one's first results in a new field are always valueless; and, in the second place, that the more an establisment is a factory, the less it is a school. No attempt has ever been made, to my knowledge, to make a school of penmanship, or English composition, or surgery, or medicine or law self-supporting.

In a manual training school, everything is for the benefit of the boy; he is the only article to be put upon the market. We can not afford to turn out anything else. Time and opportunity for growth are too precious. The moment a class has learned fairly well how to make bolts and nuts, or to cut and solder a tin funnel with an elbow in it, the boy must move on to master some new and unknown process, instead of stopping to make bolts and funnels for the market.

RELATION TO CRAFTS.

Now, as to the relation which our instruction bears to the crafts in most frequent use. During the total allowance of three hundred and eighty hours, which, in the first year, every boy of the class must devote to wood work, the boys are learning some of the preliminary steps and essential features of several wood-working trades. The sharpening of chisels, gouges, bits and planes; the filing and setting of saws; learning to square up and lay out work with precision; the cutting of mortises and tenons; the details of nailing, glueing, pinning and dovetailing; various kinds of inside and outside turning, chucking and fitting, etc., etc. All these belong equally to the cabinet maker, the chair maker, the pattern maker, the wheelwright, the house carpenter, the stair builder, the cooper, the car builder, the wood carver, and so on. While thus learning the intelligent use and care of tools and materials, our boys become very proficient in making and using what are called "working drawings." This last accomplishment is essential to intelligent progress in any trade.

The training given during the second year of school in the forging shop is equally fundamental and equally broad in its application. The study of form as related to strength and economy of material; the operations of drawing, upsetting, bending, punching, breaking, welding, tempering, brasing and soldering are fundamental in character and preparatory to a score of distinct occupations, the special business and conventional details of which we do not pretend to teach.

Our machine shop, in which the third year students spend their three hundred and eighty hours of shop time, is quite appropriately named. To be sure, there are benches where regular exercises in chipping and filing are done, but the greater part of the attention is given to the study, use and management of machines. To this end, machines with great range of adjustment, and always requiring precision and the exercise of forethought and good judgment, are employed. The materials wrought are those of which machines are generally made, viz: iron, cast and wrought, steel of various grades and brass. Their cutting tools the students generally make for themselves at the forge. We have in all twenty-one iron cutting machines, and a sixty-horse power Corliss engine. It is no small thing to be able to use all these machines intelligently, not to say skillfully, and in this age, when many new machines are to be made, and all sorts of machines are to be used in the arts, there can be no surer way than ours of devoloping that "directive power" which is generally conceded to be one of the chief fruits of a good education.

Now, whether our boys become mining, or civil, or mechanical engineers, farmers or mechanics, merchants, manufacturers, lawyers or statesmen, it seems clear that this training will give them additional power, both in moulding circumstances and in their intercourse with men, taught and untaught, skilled and unskilled.

THE COST.

A single word as to the cost. I do not recommend manual training because it is cheap, or because it will result in an immediate saving of money. In the long run, it will save much money, but its establishment and maintenance are expensive. To begin with, a building with schoolrooms and desks, drawing rooms and stands, shops and tools, costs more than one with only schoolrooms and desks. Our working sections have from twenty to twenty-four students each, and for each section there must be a teacher. In the St. Louis school, there are two hundred and thirty pupils and eleven actual teachers. Again, the current expenses of shops and laboratories are considerable. In my school, it costs from five dollars to seven dollars per pupil per year for materials. But I strongly insist that the added value is worth the added cost, and that no community in which a manual training school has once been well established would allow its expense to be an argument against it.

EVENLY-TRAINED BOYS.

I have said that the only article we put upon the market is evenly-trained boys ; I now wish to add that the article is a new one. You cannot determine its value by invoicing the boys who, in the past, have drifted without proper education and without intelligent choice into shops and offices. I do not claim that manual training will change a dull boy into a bright one, or a bad boy into a good one ; but it gives every dull boy, whether his dullness is in the direction of mathematics, or language, or mechanics, a chance to become less dull, and the bright boy a chance to retain his brilliancy. We have had some bad boys, but I honestly think their badness was less corrupting than it would have been among boys less absorbed in their work. It is not safe to reason that, because a boy cannot succeed anywhere else, he must succeed in the shop. Brains are as essential in our school as in any school ; as requisite to a thoroughly accomplished mechanic as to a good soldier or a good orator.

Doubtless more than half of our boys will find abundant uses for their manual training, and they will have a marked advantage over the untrained boys. They are all fair draughtsmen. They have a wide acquaintance with hand and machine tools, and considerable skill in their use. They have an experimental knowledge of the properties of common materials, of the marvellous effects of heat, of the nature and amount of friction. Moreover, they have a fair command of English, an excellent knowledge of elementary mathematics, and are familiar with the first principles of natural science. They have analyzed mechanical processes and learned to adapt means to ends. They have some knowledge of our literature, and generally of Latin and French grammars. Such boys will never become mere mechanic men. Do not associate them in your thoughts with that class of workmen who, aside from the stock details of a single craft, have no cultivation whatever. They will never be content, whatever the vocation to which circumstances and their own fitness may call them, to put their brains away like a piece of ornamental toggery for which they have no daily use. They have many chances in their favor. They have fast hold of a ladder which, with vigorous climbing, will carry them to the top.

HEALTHY EDUCATION.

It almost goes without saying that the varied exercises of a manual training school are highly conducive to physical health. On the intellectual and moral sides, I hope I have shown that the effect must always be good. A training which enables a boy to make the most of himself in a broad and high sense, must be regarded as healthy. A manual training school has many windows, and it looks out upon a large circle of human activities, and the kindling light shines in on every side. As with its windows, so with its doors ; its pupils step into the busy world in all directions, each choosing a career where he may be reasonably certain of success. There are many avenues to culture and to success in life—we strive to keep them all open.

The system I advocate sets up no false standards ; it does not mistake mere bookishness for generous culture. It teaches that neither the eye, nor the hand nor the head can dispense with mutual co-operation and aid. It recognizes the actual claims of our civilization. It aims to elevate, to dignify, to liberalize, all the essential elements of society ; and it renders it possible for every honorable calling to be the happy home of cultivation and refinement.

Its grand result will be an increasing interest in manufacturing pursuits, more intelligent mechanics, more successful merchants, better lawyers, more skillful physicians and more useful citizens.